004–006 DATA PROCESSING AND COMPUTER SCIENCE
AND
CHANGES IN RELATED DISCIPLINES

DDC

DEWEY Decimal Classification®

004-006 Data Processing and Computer Science and Changes in Related Disciplines

Revision of Edition 19

Prepared by

JULIANNE BEALL
Decimal Classification Specialist

with the assistance of
JOHN P. COMAROMI, Editor
DEWEY Decimal Classification

WINTON E. MATTHEWS, JR.
Decimal Classification Specialist

GREGORY R. NEW
Decimal Classification Specialist

FOREST PRESS
A Division of the
Lake Placid Education Foundation

85 WATERVLIET AVENUE
ALBANY, NEW YORK 12206 U.S.A.
1985

Library of Congress Cataloging in Publication Data

Dewey, Melvil, 1851–1931.
  DDC, Dewey decimal classification. 004–006 data
processing and computer science and changes in related
disciplines.

  Includes index.
  1. Classification, Dewey decimal. 2. Classification—
Books—Electronic data processing. 3. Classification—
Books—Computers. 4. Classification—Books—Computer
engineering. I. Beall, Julianne, 1946-   . II. Title.
III. Title: Dewey decimal classification.
Z696.D72E433 1985 /   025.4′6004   85-1667
ISBN 0-910608-36-9

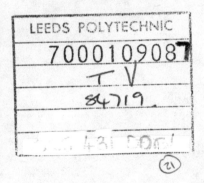

Contents

Publisher's Foreword

The publication of these new and greatly expanded schedules for computer science and computer engineering of the Dewey Decimal Classification represents the initial implementation of the policy of continuous revision recently adopted by the Forest Press Committee. In response to users of the Classification, the Committee met with the Editor and staff of the Decimal Classification Division, Library of Congress, and with members of the Editorial Policy Committee to consider the possibility of releasing *between editions* revisions and expansions in the Classification which could be applied by the Division upon publication. This policy of continuous revision will eliminate long delays between the completion of revisions and expansions and their application. It will also enable the library community to absorb smaller amounts of revision over a longer period of time since DDC editions will appear less frequently.

The members of the Forest Press Committee, Walter W. Curley, Chairman, Henry M. Bonner, Richard K. Gardner, John A. Humphry, James M. O'Brien, Thomas N. Stainback, Thomas E. Sullivan and Elaine Svenonius, wish to express appreciation to all those acknowledged by John P. Comaromi, Editor of the Dewey Decimal Classification, and Julianne Beall, Decimal Classification Specialist. Special note must be made of Julianne Beall's excellent work in the development and preparation of these revisions and expansions. She carefully and skillfully guided the schedules through various versions, incorporating constructive suggestions for improvements from many informed individuals, including members of the Editorial Policy Committee; a Subcommittee of the Subject Analysis Committee of the Cataloging and Classification Section of the American Library Association; and the (British) Library Association's Dewey Decimal Classification Committee.

It is hoped that this much needed publication will serve our users well, and that they will feel free to send comments and suggestions about it to Forest Press or the Decimal Classification Division.

John A. Humphry
EXECUTIVE DIRECTOR
Forest Press Division
Lake Placid Education Foundation

Acknowledgments

We wish to express our deep appreciation for the help, advice, and constructive criticism provided by many people at all stages in the development of the new schedules.

We received full support and cooperation from the Forest Press Committee (members' names listed in the Publisher's Foreword) and from the Decimal Classification Editorial Policy Committee: Joanne S. Anderson, Science Librarian, San Diego Public Library; Henriette D. Avram, Assistant Librarian for Processing Services, Library of Congress; Lizbeth J. Bishoff, Principal Librarian for Support Services, Pasadena Public Library; Barbara Branson, Principal Cataloger, Duke University Library; Lois M. Chan, Professor, College of Library Science, University of Kentucky; Margaret E. Cockshutt, Professor, Faculty of Library and Information Science, University of Toronto; Betty M. E. Croft, Technical Services Librarian, Northwestern Missouri State University Library; John A. Humphry, Executive Director, Forest Press; Peter J. Paulson, Director, New York State Library; Russell Sweeney, Principal Lecturer, School of Librarianship, Leeds Polytechnic; and Arnold S. Wajenberg, Principal Cataloger, University of Illinois Library at Urbana-Champaign.

Two other groups provided excellent critiques of many drafts. One was a subcommittee of the American Library Association's Subject Analysis Committee: Joan Mitchell, AT&T Bell Laboratories; Deborah Ashby, Tucson Public Library; and Lois M. Pausch, University of Illinois Library at Urbana-Champaign. The other group was the Library Association Dewey Decimal Classification Committee: Russell Sweeney, Leeds Polytechnic; Frances Hendrix, Preston Polytechnic; Chris Koster, Kensington and Chelsea Public Libraries; Martin Nail, British Library, Bibliographic Services Division; Roy Payne, Camden Public Libraries; Lis Phelan, Manchester Public Libraries; and R. Ross Trotter, British Library, Bibliographic Services Division.

Much helpful criticism came also from other sources. A group at the Library of Congress critiqued one draft: Barbara J. Roland, John R. James, and Linda Miller of the Automation Planning and Liaison Office, and Ray S. Denenberg of the Network Development Office. Many individuals critiqued one or more drafts: Pamela P. Brown, Arlington Heights Memorial Library; Pat Cholach, Hamilton Public Library; Michael D. Cramer, University of Illinois Library at Urbana-Champaign; Roy Davies, University of Exeter; D. Wyn Evans, University of Exeter; Jane Gosling, Plymouth Polytechnic; Elaine Higgins, University of Montana; Paul G. Holder, Hamilton Public Library; Malcolm Jackson, Southwark Public Libraries; Bernard L. Karon, University of Minnesota; Susi Koch, Arlington Heights Memorial Library; Brian Lantz, Birmingham Polytechnic; William Mischo, Engineering Library, University of Illinois at Urbana-Champaign; Karen J. Novak, Mindscape, Inc.; Edwin D. Reilly, Jr., Computer Science Department, State University of New York at

Albany; C. Derek Robinson, Ontario Hydro; D. M. Salter, University of Exeter; Hameed Shaikh, Hamilton Public Library; John Still, Brighton Polytechnic; Richard Weaver, New York State Library; L. White, Oxfordshire Public Libraries; and Diane J. Young, City Library, Springfield, Massachusetts.

We are grateful for the assistance of the Decimal Classification Division staff: Letitia J. Reigle, Ruth A. Sievers, Virginia Anne Schoepf, and especially Winton E. Matthews, Jr., and Gregory R. New.

We are also grateful for the support and assistance of Forest Press: John A. Humphry, Executive Director; Judith Kramer-Greene, Forest Press Editor; Mildred Gipp-Dugan, Accountant; and Judith M. Pisarski, Secretary.

John P. Comaromi, Editor
DEWEY Decimal Classification

Julianne Beall
Decimal Classification Specialist

Introduction

In response to public demand and at the recommendation of the Decimal Classification Editorial Policy Committee, Forest Press has authorized development of new and greatly expanded schedules for computer science and computer engineering to accommodate the rapid growth in these fields. To make room for expansion and to minimize the re-use of numbers, data processing and computer science have been moved from 001.6 to 004–006, and computer engineering has been moved from 621.38195 to 621.39.

004 includes the generalities of data processing and computer science; selection and use of computer hardware and computer systems; and processing modes.

005 deals with computer programming, programs, and data. Both software and firmware and their development are covered in this section.

006 treats special computer methods, such as artificial intelligence, pattern recognition, and computer graphics.

The computer engineering schedule at 621.39 is patterned after 004, with a section at the end analogous to 006.

In addition to these new sections, which have been presented in schedule format, related but scattered changes have been presented in the format of *Decimal Classification Additions, Notes, and Decisions (DC&)*. For example, the numbers previously divided like 001.6 (standard subdivision −0285, 651.8, and 658.05) have been revised to match the new schedule. A new set of numbers for computer communications has been developed at 384.3.

The editors have also provided an index to the new numbers and related numbers in Edition 19, a manual of application, and a glossary. All have entries pertinent to both the schedule and *DC&* parts of this publication. The glossary has been included to let the classifier know which definition of a word is being used for the schedule, because the terminology in computer science and related fields is currently in flux. Once the terminology in these fields has stabilized, the glossary will be dropped. Because previously there were so few computer numbers by comparison with those now available, comparative and equivalence tables have not been deemed useful and have not been provided.

John P. Comaromi, Editor
DEWEY Decimal Classification

Julianne Beall
Decimal Classification Specialist

004   Data processing   Computer science

This schedule (004–006), which replaces that formerly appearing at 001.6, is new.

Class here selection and use of computer hardware; comprehensive works on hardware and programs in electronic data processing; electronic computers; electronic digital computers; computer systems (computers, their peripheral devices, their operating systems); central processing units; computer reliability; general computer performance evaluation

Unless other instructions are given, class complex subjects with aspects in two or more subdivisions of 004 in the one coming last, e.g., external storage for microcomputers 004.56 (*not* 004.16)

Class systems programs in 005.43; engineering of computers in 621.39; data processing and computer science applied to a specific subject or discipline with the subject or discipline, using "Standard Subdivisions" notation 0285 from Table 1, e.g., data processing in banking 332.10285

> *For computer programming, programs, data, see 005; special computer methods, 006*
>
> *See also 001.434 for computer simulation and modeling in research; 025.04 for information storage and retrieval; 346.07 for legal aspects of the use of computers in industry and trade; 364.168 for financial and business computer crimes; 371.39445 for computer-assisted instruction (CAI); 652.5 for word processing; 658.05 for data processing in management; 794.82 for computer games*
>
> *See Manual at 004–006 vs. 621.39; 004 vs. 005*

.015 1   Mathematical principles

> Class here computer mathematics [*formerly* 519.4]

.019   Human-computer interaction

> Class here psychological principles and human factors in data processing and computer science
>
> *For ergonomic engineering of computer peripherals, see 621.3984*
>
> *See Manual at 004.019*

.02   Miscellany

.021 8   Standards

> *See Manual at 004.0218*

.028   Techniques, procedures, apparatus, equipment, materials

[.028 7]   Testing and measurement

> Do not use; class in 004.24

.068   Management of data processing, of computer science

> *See Manual at 004.068*

1

SUMMARY

.1   General works on specific types of computers

Class here specific types of processors, computer systems based on specific types of computers

Class programmable calculators in 510.28541; specific types of computers, processors, computer systems distinguished by their processing modes in 004.3

See Manual at 004.1

> ### 004.11–004.16   Digital computers

Class comprehensive works in 004

See Manual at 004.11–004.16

.11   Digital supercomputers

.12   Digital mainframe computers

Class here large-scale digital computers

For supercomputers, see 004.11

.125   Specific digital mainframe computers

Arrange alphabetically by name of computer or processor, e.g., IBM 360®

.14   Digital minicomputers

Class comprehensive works on digital minicomputers and microcomputers in 004.16

.145   Specific digital minicomputers

Arrange alphabetically by name of minicomputer or processor, e.g., HP/1000®

.16   Digital microcomputers

Including pocket computers capable of manipulating alphabetic as well as numeric data

Class here personal computers, comprehensive works on minicomputers and microcomputers

.165 Specific digital microcomputers

Arrange alphabetically by name of microcomputer or microprocessor, e.g., Apple II®

.19 Hybrid and analogue computers

For non-electronic analogue computers, see 004.9

.2 Systems analysis and design, computer architecture, performance evaluation

.21 Systems analysis and design

Class here analysis of a user's problem preparatory to developing a computer system to solve it

Class commmunications network design and architecture in 004.65

For database design and architecture, see 005.74

See also 003 for interdisciplinary works on systems analysis and design, 658.4032 for management use of systems analysis

See Manual at 004.21 vs. 003; 004.21 vs. 004.22 and 621.392

.22 Computer architecture

See Manual at 004.21 vs. 004.22 and 621.392

.24 Performance evaluation

Class here performance measurement and evaluation to aid in designing or improving the performance of a computer system

Class performance evaluation as a consideration in purchasing in 004.029

See Manual at 004.24

.25 Systems analysis and design, computer architecture, performance evaluation of specific types of electronic computers

Add to base number 004.25 the numbers following 004.1 in 004.11–004.19, e.g., architecture of digital microcomputers 004.256

.3 Processing modes

Including batch, offline, pipeline processing

Class here computers, processors, computer systems distinguished by their processing modes; centralized processing

.32 Multiprogramming

Class here time sharing

.33   Real-time processing

Class here online and interactive processing

Class interactive processing in databases in 005.74, in special computer methods in 006

.35   Multiprocessing

Including associative processing

Class here parallel processing

Class comprehensive works on associative processing and memory in 004.5

.36   Distributed processing

See also 004.6 for computer communications networks, 005.758 for distributed databases

.5   Storage

Including comprehensive works on associative (content-addressable) memory and associative processing

Class associative processing in 004.35

.53   Internal storage (Main memory)

Examples: magnetic-core, metal-oxide-semiconductor (MOS), semiconductor bipolar, thin-film memory; random-access memory (RAM); read-only memory (ROM)

See also 005.6 for microprogramming and microprograms

.54   Virtual memory

.56   External (Auxiliary) storage

Examples: hard and floppy disks; magnetic tapes, e.g., cartridges, cassettes, reel-to-reel tapes; tape and disk drives; magnetic bubble memory; optical storage devices; punched cards

.6   Interfacing and communications

Equipment and techniques linking computers to peripheral devices or to other computers

Class here interdisciplinary works on computer communications

Class data, programs, programming in interfacing and communications in 005.7; social aspects of computer communications in 302.23; economic and related aspects of providing computer communications to the public in 384.3

See also 004.36 for distributed processing

See Manual at 004.6; 004.6 vs. 005.71; 384.3 vs. 004.6

[.602 18]   Standards

> Do not use; class in 004.62

.61   For specific types of electronic computers

> Add to base number 004.61 the numbers following 004.1 in 004.11–004.19, e.g., interfacing and communications for microcomputers 004.616

.62   Interfacing and communications protocols (standards)

> Class protocols for specific aspects of interfacing and communications with the aspect, e.g., protocols for error-correcting codes 005.72

[.620 218]   Standards

> Do not use; class in 004.62

.64   Various specific kinds of hardware

> Examples: baseband and broadband equipment, modems, optical-fiber cable, peripheral control units

> Class peripheral control units controlling a specific kind of peripheral with the peripheral, e.g., printer controllers 004.77

> 004.65–004.68 Computer communications networks

> Class comprehensive works in 004.6

.65   Communications network architecture

> Class here systems analysis, design, topology (configuration) of computer communications networks

.66   Data transmission modes and data switching methods

> Including circuit and packet switching, multiplexing

.67   Wide-area networks

.68   Local-area networks

> Including baseband and broadband local-area networks, high-speed local networks

.7   **Peripherals**

> Input, output, storage devices that work with a computer but are not part of its central processing unit or internal storage

> Class peripheral storage in 004.56

> *See also 004.64 for communications devices*

.71   For specific types of electronic computers

> Add to base number 004.71 the numbers following 004.1 in 004.11–004.19, e.g., peripherals for microcomputers 004.716

.75   Peripherals combining input and output functions

Class here computer terminals

Class tape and disk devices in 004.56

.76   Input peripherals

Examples: card readers, keyboards

Class input devices that utilize pattern recognition methods in 006.4; special-purpose input devices with the purpose, e.g., graphics input devices 006.62, game paddles 688.748

See also 005.72 for data entry

.77   Output peripherals

Examples: computer output microform (COM) devices, monitors (video display screens), printers

Class output peripherals that utilize computer sound synthesis in 006.5, computer graphics output devices in 006.62

See also 005.43 for monitors in the sense of software control programs, 005.6 for monitors in the sense of firmware control programs

.9   Non-electronic data processing

General concepts: automatic and nonautomatic

Including non-electronic punched-card data processing, e.g., pre-computer use of Hollerith cards; non-electronic analogue computers

Class comprehensive works on analogue computers in 004.19

005   Computer programming, programs, data

Class here text processing; software reliability, compatibility, portability

Unless other instructions are given, class complex subjects with aspects in two or more subdivisions of 005 in the one coming last, e.g., designing structured FORTRAN programs 005.133 (*not* 005.113 or 005.12)

Class computer programming, programs, data for special computer methods in 006

See also 652.5 for word processing

See Manual at 004 vs. 005; 005

SUMMARY

005.1   **Programming**
.2   **Programming for specific types of computers**
.3   **Programs**
.4   **Systems programming and programs**
.6   **Microprogramming and microprograms**
.7   **Data in computer systems**
.8   **Data security**

> **005.1–005.6 Computer programming and programs**

    Class comprehensive works in 005

.1 **Programming**

    Class here software engineering, application programming

    Class a specific application of programming within computer science with the application in 005.4–006.6

      For programming for specific types of computers, see 005.2

      See Manual at 005.1 vs. 005.3; 005.1 vs. 510

.102 8   Techniques, procedures, apparatus, equipment, materials

    Class special techniques in 005.11

[.102 87]   Testing and measurement

    Do not use; class in 005.14

[.102 88]   Maintenance and repair

    Do not use; class in 005.16

.11   Special programming techniques

    See Manual at 005.11

.112   Modular programming

.113   Structured programming

.12   Program design

.120 28   Techniques, procedures, apparatus, equipment, materials

    See Manual at 005.12028

.13   Programming languages

    Including application generators, nonprocedural languages

    Class here coding of programs

    See also 005.43 for job-control languages

[.130 151]   Mathematical principles

    Do not use; class in 005.131

.131   Symbolic (Mathematical) logic

    Class here mathematical principles of programming languages, e.g., formal languages and grammars applied to programming languages

    See Manual at 005.131

.133 **Specific programming languages**

Class here comprehensive works on programming with specific programming languages

Arrange alphabetically by name of programming language, e.g., COBOL

Class specific machine and assembly languages in 005.136, specific microprogramming languages in 005.6

See also 005.45 for programming-language translators for specific programming languages

.136 **Machine and assembly languages**

Class here comprehensive works on programming with machine and assembly languages

See Manual at 005.136

.14 **Verification, testing, measurement, debugging**

.15 **Preparation of program documentation**

Class here software documentation

See also 005.3 for program documentation itself, 808.066005 for technical writing in preparation of program documentation

See Manual at 005.15

.16 **Program maintenance**

Class here software maintenance

.2 Programming for specific types of computers

Add to base number 005.2 the numbers following 004.1 in 004.11–004.19, e.g., programming digital microcomputers 005.26

See Manual at 005.136

.3 Programs

Software and firmware

Collections of programs, systems of interrelated programs, individual programs having interdisciplinary applications

General concepts: history, description, critical appraisal, selection, use

Class here application programs, software documentation

Class programs for a specific application in computer science with the application in 005–006

For firmware, see 005.6

See also 005.15 for preparation of program documentation

See Manual at 005.1 vs. 005.3; 005.3

.302 18   Standards

> See also 005.10218 for standards for programming, 005.150218 for standards for preparation of software documentation
>
> See Manual at 005.1 vs. 005.3

.302 87   Testing and measurement

> See also 005.14 for testing and measurement in programming
>
> See Manual at 005.1 vs. 005.3

[.302 88]   Maintenance and repair

> Do not use; class in 005.16

> 005.31–005.36   For digital computers

Class comprehensive works in 005.3

.31   For digital supercomputers

.32   For digital mainframe computers

.322   In specific programming languages

> Arrange alphabetically by name of programming language, e.g., COBOL
>
> See Manual at 005.322

.325   For specific computers

> Class here programs for specific processors, programs for computer systems based on specific computers
>
> Arrange alphabetically by name of computer or processor, e.g., Burroughs B6700®

.329   Specific programs

> Class here specific computer software systems (organized sets of programs that work together)
>
> Arrange alphabetically by name of program or software system, e.g., SAS
>
> See Manual at 005.329

.34   For digital minicomputers

> Add to base number 005.34 the numbers following 005.32 in 005.322–005.329, e.g., programs for the PDP-11® 005.345

.36   For digital microcomputers

> Add to base number 005.36 the numbers following 005.32 in 005.322–005.329, e.g., programs for the AT&T Personal Computer® 005.365

.39   For hybrid and analogue computers

.4   Systems programming and programs

Class programming and programs for interfacing and data communications in 005.71, for management of files and databases in 005.74

.42   Systems programming

Class here programming for operating systems

Class programming for specific aspects of operating systems with the aspect, e.g., programming for communications 005.71; programming for other specific kinds of systems programs with the kind, e.g., programming for compilers 005.453

.43   Systems programs   Operating systems

Including job-control languages, programs for multiprogramming and virtual memory, utility programs

Class programming for operating systems in 005.42; a specific application of systems programs with the application, e.g., programs that aid in debugging other programs 005.14, programming-language translators 005.45, text editors 652.5

For operating systems for specific types of computers, see 005.44

See Manual at 005.43

.44   Operating systems for specific types of computers   *DON'T use*

use .43

Add to base number 005.44 the numbers following 005.3 in 005.31–005.39, e.g., operating systems for digital microcomputers 005.446

.45   Programming-language translators

Including interpreters

Class here code generators, macro processors, parsers, translators for specific programming languages

Class translators for microprogramming languages in 005.6

See also 418.02 for programs to translate natural languages into other natural languages

.453   Compilers

.456   Assemblers

.6   Microprogramming and microprograms

Including firmware viewed as microprograms, firmware development, microassembly languages, microcode

Class firmware viewed as hardware in 004

See Manual at 005.6

.7   Data in computer systems

> *For data security, see 005.8*

.71   Data communications

> Including programs and programming for interfacing and data communications
>
> Class here interfacing
>
> > *See also 004.6 for hardware for interfacing and data communications*
> >
> > *See Manual at 004.6; 004.6 vs. 005.71; 005.71*

.72   Data representation and preparation

> Including conversion to machine-readable form; data entry and validation; digital codes, e.g., ASCII; error-correcting codes
>
> Class data validation in file processing in 005.74, computer input devices in 004.76
>
> > *For data encryption and ciphers, see 005.82*

.73   Data structures

.74   Data files and databases

> Including data validation in file processing
>
> Class here file structures (file organizations), file processing, file and database management systems, database design and architecture
>
> Class comprehensive works on data validation in 005.72; data files and databases with regard to their subject content with the subject, e.g., encyclopedic databases 030, non-bibliographic medical databases 610
>
> > *For specific types of data files and databases, see 005.75*
> >
> > *See also 025.04 for information storage and retrieval systems*
> >
> > *See Manual at 005.74*

.740 1–.740 5   Standard subdivisions of data files, of databases

.740 6   Organizations and management of data files, of databases

.740 68   Management of data files, of databases

> > *See Manual at 005.74068*

.740 7–.740 9   Standard subdivisions of data files, of databases

.742   Data dictionaries/directories

> Class here data dictionaries, data directories

.746   Data compression (File compression, Data compaction)

.748	Sorting

Class here merging

.75	Specific types of data files and databases ·

Including centralized files and databases, hierarchical databases

.754	Network databases

Including database management systems that conform to the standards developed by CODASYL (Conference on Data Systems Languages)

.756	Relational databases

.756 5	Specific relational database management systems

Arrange alphabetically by name of database management system, e.g., dBASE II®

.758	Distributed data files and databases

See also 004.36 for distributed processing

.8	**Data security**

Class here access control

See also 658.478 for data security in management

.82	Data encryption

Class here ciphers

See Manual at 005.82 vs. 652.8

006   Special computer methods

Not otherwise provided for

Class here programs, programming, selection and use of hardware in relation to special computer methods

Class computer modeling and simulation in research in 001.434, in research in a specific discipline or subject with the discipline or subject, using "Standard Subdivisions" notation 0724 from Table 1, e.g., computer simulation in economics research 330.0724; computer communications in 004.6; file and database management in 005.74; special computer methods in automatic control engineering in 629.89

For data security, see 005.8

.3   Artificial intelligence [*formerly* 001.535]

Class here question-answering systems

Unless other instructions are given, class complex subjects with aspects in two or more subdivisions of 006.3 in the one coming last, e.g., natural language processing in expert systems 006.35 (*not* 006.33)

See also 006.4 for pattern recognition

.31   Machine learning

.33   Knowledge-based systems

> Class here expert systems

.35   Natural language processing

> Computer processing of natural language used to allow people to communicate with computers in natural language instead of through formalized commands

> > *See also 402.85 for computer processing of natural language as a tool in linguistics*

.37   Computer vision

> > *See also 006.42 for optical pattern recognition*

> > *See Manual at 006.37 vs. 006.42, 621.367, 621.391, and 621.399*

.4   **Pattern recognition [*formerly also* 001.534]**

> Class pattern recognition in artificial intelligence in 006.3

.42   Optical pattern recognition

> Including bar-code scanning and scanners, perceptrons

> Class optical engineering aspects of optical pattern recognition in 621.367

> > *See also 006.37 for computer vision*

> > *See Manual at 006.37 vs. 006.42, 621.367, 621.391, and 621.399*

.424   Optical character recognition (OCR) [*formerly also* 001.534]

> Including optical-character scanning and scanners

.45   Acoustical pattern recognition

.454   Speech recognition

> Including speaker recognition

> Class here comprehensive works on speech recognition and speech synthesis

> > *For speech synthesis, see 006.54*

.5   **Computer sound synthesis**

> > *See also 789.99 for computer music*

.54   Speech synthesis

.6   **Computer graphics**

Class here comprehensive works on computer graphics and computer sound synthesis

For computer sound synthesis, see 006.5

See also 760 for computer art

.62   Hardware

Examples: digitizer tablets, graphics terminals, plotters

See Manual at 006.62

.66   Programming

Including graphics programming languages

For programming for specific types of computers, see 006.67

.67   Programming for specific types of computers

Add to base number 006.67 the numbers following 004.1 in 004.11–004.19, e.g., graphics programming for digital microcomputers 006.676

.68   Programs

Add to base number 006.68 the numbers following 005.3 in 005.31–005.39, e.g., graphics programs for digital microcomputers 006.686

.39   Computers

> This schedule, which replaces that formerly appearing at 621.38195, is new.
>
> Class here electronic digital computers, central processing units, computer reliability, general computer performance evaluation
>
> Unless other instructions are given, class complex subjects with aspects in two or more subdivisions of 621.39 in the one coming last, e.g., circuitry of computer internal storage in 621.3973 (*not* 621.395)
>
> Class selection and use of computer hardware, works treating both hardware and either programming or programs in 004; specific applications with the subject, e.g., use of computers to regulate processes automatically 629.895
>
> *See Manual at 004–006 vs. 621.39; 621.39*

[.390 287]   Testing and measurement

> Do not use; class in 621.392

.391   General works on specific types of computers

> Including optical computers
>
> Class here specific types of processors, e.g., multiprocessors
>
> *For programmable calculators, see 681.14*
>
> *See Manual at 006.37 vs. 006.42, 621.367, 621.391, and 621.399*

>   621.391 1–621.391 6   Digital computers

> Class comprehensive works in 621.39
>
> *See Manual at 004.11–004.16*

.391 1   Digital supercomputers

.391 2   Digital mainframe computers

> *For digital supercomputers, see 621.3911*

.391 4   Digital minicomputers

> Class comprehensive works on digital minicomputers and microcomputers in 621.3916

.391 6   Digital microcomputers

> Class here personal computers, comprehensive works on minicomputers and microcomputers

.391 9   Hybrid and analogue computers

.392   Systems analysis and design, computer architecture, performance evaluation

>*See Manual at 004.21 vs. 004.22 and 621.392*

.395   Circuitry

>Class here logic circuits, logic design of circuitry, very-large-scale integration (VLSI)

>Class comprehensive works on logic circuits in 621.381537, on microelectronic circuits in 621.38173

>*See Manual at 621.395 vs. 621.38173*

.397   Storage

.397 3   Internal storage (Main memory)

>Including magnetic-core and thin-film memory

>Class here random-access memory (RAM), read-only memory (ROM)

.397 32   Semiconductor memory

>Including bipolar and metal-oxide-semiconductor (MOS) memory

.397 6   External (Auxiliary) storage

>Including hard and floppy disks; magnetic tapes, e.g., cartridges, cassettes, reel-to-reel tapes; tape and disk drives

.397 63   Magnetic bubble memory

.397 67   Optical storage devices

>Class storage of pictorial data in optical storage devices in 621.367

.398   Interfacing and communications devices, peripherals

.398 1   Interfacing and communications devices

>*See Manual at 004.6*

.398 14   Analogue-to-digital and digital-to-analogue converters

>Example: modems

.398 4   Peripherals

>Class here ergonomic engineering of computer peripherals

>Class peripheral storage in 621.3976

>*For peripherals combining input and output functions, see 621.3985; input peripherals, 621.3986; output peripherals, 621.3987*

16

.398 5   Peripherals combining input and output functions

Class here computer terminals

Class tape and disk devices in 621.3976

.398 6   Input peripherals

Examples: card readers, keyboards

.398 7   Output peripherals

Examples: computer output microform (COM) devices, monitors (video display screens), printers

See also 621.399 for computer graphics

.399   Devices for special computer methods

Including computer graphics, pattern recognition

See Manual at 006.37 vs. 006.42, 621.367, 621.391, and 621.399

Index

Manual of Application

—0151 vs.
—0285   **[Mathematical principles] vs. Data processing Computer applications**

Mathematics applied to a discipline or subject is classed with the discipline or subject, using s.s. 0151; and data processing applied to a discipline or subject is classed with the discipline or subject, using s.s. 0285. Mathematics may be applied to data processing, and data processing may be applied to mathematics.

A. Class mathematics applied to data processing in 004–006, using s.s. 0151, e.g., recursive functions used to explain how computers work 004.015113. Class comprehensive works on mathematical concepts in 510, e.g., recursive functions 511.3.

B. Class data processing applied to mathematics in 510, using s.s. 0285, e.g., computer programs to solve differential equations 515.35028553. Class comprehensive works on data processing concepts in 004–006, e.g., computer programs 005.3.

—0285   **Data processing Computer applications**

It is redundant to add only the digit *4* to —0285, since —02854 would mean applied data processing and computer science, the same as —0285; hence —02854 is never used by itself. If the applied concept is one that would be classed in 004 were it unapplied, do not add anything to —0285, e.g., digital computers applied to a subject —285. It is not redundant, however, to add *4* plus additional digits to —0285, e.g., digital microcomputers applied to a subject —0285416. It is not redundant to add only the digits *5* or *6* to —0285, e.g., applied computer programming, programs, data —02855.

It is similarly redundant to add only the digit *4* to 651.8 Data processing Computer applications [in office services] and 658.05 Data processing Computer applications [in management], since 651.84 and 658.054 would mean the same thing as 651.8 and 658.05.

Do not use —0285 and its subdivisions with numbers that already specify or imply data processing, computer science, computer communications, or applications of these. Terms like *automation* or *mechanized* frequently occur in connection with these numbers. For example:

025.04   Information storage and retrieval systems

Class here comprehensive works on mechanized storage, search, retrieval of information by libraries and other information services

629.2549 Electronic systems [of internal combustion engines in motor land vehicles] (Nearly all such electronic systems now involve computers.)

670.427   Mechanization and automation of factory operations

Machine-readable materials and programs

Do not use −0285 to indicate that a work is in machine-readable form (e.g., do not use it for census data stored on machine-readable tapes). −028 (Techniques, procedures, apparatus, equipment, materials) is not to be used as a form subdivision. A program, however, may be regarded as a kind of apparatus—a device to make a computer work properly or to accomplish a particular user task—and works about programs typically discuss techniques and procedures. Hence −028553 and its subdivisions should be used for programs themselves and works about programs, regardless of form (e.g., programs in machine-readable form, such as disk or tape, and printed program listings bound into books).

Do not use −028553 for items that include both programs and data files, unless the data files are clearly of minor importance (e.g., small data files intended merely to help beginners learn to use the programs).

If in doubt, do not use −028553.

See also −0151 vs. −0285; 004−006 vs. 621.39.

−0285 vs. −068 **Data processing   Computer applications vs. Management of enterprises engaged in specific fields of activity, of specific kinds of enterprises**

Class the management of applied data processing with the application, using −0285, which takes precedence over −068 when management is applied to data processing. Be aware, though, that books more commonly treat data processing applied to management, in which case −068 takes precedence over −0285, e.g., data processing applied to the management of hospitals 362.11068.

003 Systems

See 004.21 vs. 003.

004−006 vs. 621.39 **[Data processing   Computer science] vs. [Engineering of] Computers**

Works classed in 004−006 treat (a) computer hardware from the user's viewpoint and/or (b) software or firmware. Works classed in 621.39 (a) treat computer hardware solely from the viewpoint of engineering or manufacturing and (b) do not treat software or the program aspect of firmware. A work treating the physical processes of manufacturing firmware chips, not discussing the programs embodied in those chips, would be classed in 621.39. Comprehensive works on the computer science and computer engineering aspects of a subject are classed in 004–006.

Works treating 004–006 concepts may be classed in 621.39 only if the 004–006 concepts are applied to 621.39 concepts, as in computer graphics programs to assist in design of computer circuitry 621.3950285668.

621.39 parallels 004 in structure, except for 621.399, which is analogous to 006. Because certain numbers in 621.39 were skipped to minimize reuse of numbers, the parallel to 004 is not as close as it would otherwise be.

Computers in general; comprehensive works on digital computers	004	621.39
Digital supercomputers	004.11	621.3911
Digital mainframe computers	004.12	621.3912
Digital minicomputers	004.14	621.3914
Digital microcomputers	004.16	621.3916
Hybrid and analogue computers	004.19	621.3919
Systems analysis and design, computer architecture, performance evaluation	004.2	621.392
Storage	004.5	621.397
Interfacing and communications	004.6	621.3981
Peripherals	004.7	621.3984
Special computer methods	006	621.399

There is no analogue for 004.3 Processing modes in 621.39 because most works focusing on processing modes include treatment of software or the program aspect of firmware and thus are not classed in 621.39. Class general works on the engineering of computers, processors (central processing units), computer systems distinguished by their processing modes in 621.391, specific aspects of such machinery with the aspect, e.g., engineering design of multiprocessors 621.392.

Most works on computer architecture and computer performance evaluation include treatment of software or the program aspect of firmware; hence there are separate subdivisions of 004.2 for these topics (004.22 Computer architecture and 004.24 Performance evaluation), but no such separate subdivisions of 621.392. Works on these topics that truly are limited to computer engineering, however, are classed at 621.392.

Engineering of devices for the special computer methods named in 006 is to be classed in 621.399, whether the devices or methods are named there or not.

There is no analogue in 004 for 621.395 Circuitry because circuitry is strictly an engineering aspect of computers, not something that the computer user needs to understand.

Computer engineering is not part of s.s. 0285. It is, however, subject to the same rule that applies to electronic engineering in general: a specific application is classed with the subject, e.g., electronic engineering of computers in robots 629.892.

004 vs. 005	**Data processing Computer science vs. Computer programming, programs, data**

Class in 004 works on computer hardware and works treating both computer hardware and the "soft" aspects of computer systems—programs, programming, and data. Class works treating only these "soft" aspects in 005. Exception: Class hardware applied to topics named in 005 with the topic using s.s. 028, e.g., database machines 005.74028. Exception to the exception: Class hardware for interfacing and data communications in 004.64 (not 005.71).

004.019   Human-computer interaction

Here the meaning of s.s. 019 has been broadened slightly to include comprehensive works on psychological and non-psychological aspects of human-computer interaction. Use s.s. 019 with its broadened meaning wherever applicable in 004–006, e.g., human factors in interactive systems 004.33019.

004.0218   Standards [in data processing, computer science]

Class here comprehensive works on standards in data processing, in computer science. Class standards applied to a particular topic with the topic, using s.s. 0218, e.g., standards for programming languages 005.130218. Exception: Class comprehensive works on standards applied to computer interfacing and communications in 004.62 without s.s. 0218.

004.068   **Management of data processing, of computer science**

Class here comprehensive works on the management of electronic data processing. Class management of particular aspects of data processing with the aspect using s.s. 068, e.g., management of computer software development 005.1068.

004.1   **General works on specific types of computers**

In this number, its subdivisions, and analogous numbers elsewhere in 004–006 and 621.39, computers and processors (central processing units) are treated for classification purposes as if they were the same. In fact they are not, but few works about processors can avoid discussing the other parts of the computer with which the processor must interact; hence works about specific types of computers and processors are typically not different enough to justify separate numbers.

Programmable calculators are classed in 510.28541 rather than 004.1 because they are limited function computers, capable of working only with numbers, not alphabetic data.

004.11–   **Digital computers**
004.16
Use these numbers and the analogous engineering numbers (621.3911–621.3916) with caution: use them only for works that emphasize the specific type of computer, not for works that may refer most of the time to a particular type as an illustration of what computers in general do. For example, use 004, not 004.12, for a general introduction to computers written at a time when the only computers were mainframes. If in doubt, prefer 004 or 621.39 without subdivision.

Supercomputers are the largest, fastest, most powerful, most expensive computers; mainframe computers are next; then minicomputers; finally microcomputers are the smallest, slowest, least powerful and least expensive computers. Specific distinctions among these types of computers have been made, especially in terms of word size, memory size, and speed; but the distinctions vary from authority to authority, manufacturer to manufacturer, and especially over time. Class a particular computer according to the way it is presented in the first work about it that a library acquires (unless it is known that that work presents an atypical view of the computer).

Do not class a work treating more than one computer or processor in a number for specific computers in 004–006 unless:

1. the work treats a single series of very closely related computers or processors (e.g., the IBM 370® series of mainframe computers 004.125 or the Intel 8080® and 8080A® microprocessors 004.165); or

2. the work treats primarily one specfic computer or processor but adds that it is also applicable to other similar machines (e.g., a work about programming the IBM PC® that says it can also be used as a guide to programming "IBM-compatible" computers 005.265).

Note: A work that discusses a computer and its processor is in ·effect a work about the computer and should be treated as such (e.g., a work about the Apple II® computer and the 6502® microprocessor 004.165).

In case of doubt, do not use a number for specific computers.

004.21 vs. 003

Systems analysis and design vs. Systems

In addition to the analysis and design of computer-based systems, class in 004.21 and s.s. 0285421 systems analysis in the sense of analyzing a user's problem in order to design a computer-based system to solve it. Class a work on systems analysis and design that is not concerned primarily with computer-based systems in 003 or with the specific system.

004.21 vs. 004.22 and 621.392

Systems analysis and design vs. Computer architecture [and] Systems analysis and design, computer architecture, performance evaluation [in computer engineering]

In 004.21 systems analysis and design of a computer-based system involves a computer, application programs, and procedures, usually also other hardware, often a database and communications network, all working together to accomplish a task for the user. *Computer architecture* in 004.22 focuses on the design and structure of the computer itself and on the computer in relation to its peripheral devices. Most works on computer architecture treat software or the program aspect of firmware as well as hardware; but in the discussion of programs, the focus is on system programs, which make the computer function properly, rather than on application programs, which accomplish user tasks.

In 621.392 are classed works that treat computer hardware but do not treat software or firmware.

004.22

Computer architecture

See 004–006 vs. 621.39; 004.21 vs. 004.22 and 621.392.

004.24

Performance evaluation

Class here only specialized works treating performance measurement and evaluation as an aid in designing or improving the performance of a computer system. Class general evaluations of computers in the appropriate general works number, e.g., general evaluations of microcomputers 004.16, of the BBC Microcomputer® 004.165. If in doubt, prefer the general works number. Add s.s. 029 to the general works number if the emphasis is on evaluation as a consideration in purchasing, e.g., buyers' guides to microcomputers 004.16029.

004.6   **Interfacing and communications**

It is impossible to make a distinction useful for classification between computer interfacing and computer communications. For example, there are many similarities between (a) the interfacing techniques that link a computer and a printer located next to it and (b) the communications techniques that link a computer and a physically remote printer, terminal, or other computer. The schedule is designed so that the classifier need not distinguish computer interfacing from computer communications. In 004.6, 005.71, and 621.3981, computer interfacing and computer communications are classed in the same numbers. At these numbers, standard subdivisions may be added for works on either interfacing or communications.

See also 384.3 vs. 004.6.

004.6 vs.   **Interfacing and communications** vs. Data communications
005.71

These two numbers are parallel: interfacing is classed in both, and *computer communications* and *data communications* are synonyms. Class in 004.6 selection and use of computer interfacing and communications equipment—"hard" aspects. Class in 005.71 comprehensive works on "soft" aspects—programming, programs, and data in interfacing and communications—and works focusing specifically on programming and programs. (Class specific data aspects of interfacing and communications with the aspect in 005.7–005.8, e.g., error-correcting codes 005.72, data compression 005.746, data encryption 005.82.) Class comprehensive works on both the "hard" and "soft" aspects of computer interfacing and communications in 004.6.

005   **Computer programming, programs, data**

Beware: text processing as classed here is broader than word processing; it includes all computer processing of information coded as characters or sequences of characters (as contrasted with information coded as numbers), e.g., counting word frequency, making concordances, storing and retrieving text, sorting lists alphabetically. Class specific applications of text processing with the application, e.g., alphabetic sorting 005.748, word processing 652.5.

See also 004 vs. 005.

005.1 vs.   **Programming vs. Programs**
005.3

Class in 005.1 and other programming numbers works on programming to achieve reliability, compatibility, portability, and other ideal qualities. Class in 005.3 and other numbers for programs works that discuss whether existing programs actually have these qualities.

Class in 005.10218 and 005.150218 standards for programs and program documentation that are aimed at programmers and documentation writers, to ensure that they produce good programs and documentation. Class in 005.30218 and other numbers for programs works that discuss standards to help users in selecting from among existing programs and documentation.

Class in 005.14 testing and measurement as part of program development. Class in 005.30287 and other numbers for programs works that discuss ways for users to test or measure programs as an aid in selection.

Class a work devoted equally to programming and programs in 005.1 Programming or 005.2 Programming for specific types of computers.

005.1 vs.
510

[Computer] Programming vs. Mathematics

Certain terms may be used for both a computer-science concept and a mathematics concept. *Algorithm,* for example, may be used for processes to solve mathematical problems—with or without the aid of a computer. *Algorithm* may also be used in the context of computer programming for processes to solve many different kinds of problems—information retrieval and word-processing problems, for example, as well as mathematical problems.

Programming may refer to a branch of applied mathematics that has no necessary connection with computers, though computations necessary for this branch are commonly accomplished with the aid of a computer. For example, *linear programming* refers to the study of maximizing or minimizing a linear function $f(x_1 \ldots, x_n)$ subject to given constraints which are linear inequalities involving the variables of x_i. *Nonlinear programming* refers to the study of maximizing or minimizing a function of several variables, when the variables are constrained to yield values of other functions lying in a certain range, and either the function to be maximized or minimized, or at least one of the functions whose value is constrained, is nonlinear. Works on programming as a branch of applied mathematics are classed in 519.7. *Programming* may also refer to writing instructions to direct the operation of a computer or its peripheral equipment. Programming in this sense is classed in 005.1.

005.11

Special programming techniques

Class here special programming techniques as applied to the multiple phases of programming, e.g., works on structured programming that treat program design, coding, and testing 005.113. Class special programming techniques applied to only one phase of programming with the phase, e.g., works on structured program design 005.12.

005.12028   [Program design] Techniques, procedures, apparatus, equipment, materials

> Including the use of flowcharts and flowcharting as aids in program design. Class the preparation of flowcharts as program documentation to help other computer professionals understand programs in 005.15028. Class flowcharts and flowcharting elsewhere as appropriate, using s.s. 028, e.g., flowcharting in computer system analysis and design 004.21028.

005.131   Symbolic (Mathematical) logic [of programming languages]

> Only one branch of 510 Mathematics is frequently applied to programming languages: 511.3 Symbolic (Mathematical) logic. This branch includes such topics as formal languages, grammars, automata, and recursive functions.

> Class the mathematical principles of programming languages applied to the development of programming-language translators in 005.45, e.g., formal-language theory applied to development of compilers 005.453015113.

005.136   Machine and assembly languages

> Most machine and assembly languages are limited to a specific computer or processor (or at least to a specific type); and most works about specific machine and assembly languages emphasize programming with these languages; hence most works about specific machine and assembly languages are classed in 005.2 Programming for specific types of computers. A work about a specific machine or assembly language that did not emphasize programming would be classed here. Most of the works classed here treat machine or assembly languages in general.

005.15   Preparation of program documentation

> Class here comprehensive works on how to prepare program documentation; works on how to prepare the technical documentation needed by the personnel who will maintain, modify, and enhance the program (including such things as program source listings, program comments, flowcharts, decision logic tables, file specifications, program function descriptions, program test history records, modification logs); works on how to prepare program users' manuals that focus on content rather than form; works on policies for program documentation.

> Class preparation of program design specifications and other technical documentation as an aid in program design in 005.12.

> Class in 808.066005 works that emphasize effective technical writing — that is, works that emphasize such things as organizing for clarity, writing appropriately for the intended audience, using good para-

graph structure, preferring the active voice, using consistent terminology. Typically such works are concerned only with users' manuals. Class program documentation itself with the program in 005.3 or wherever the program is classed.

005.2   Programming for specific types of computers

See 005.136.

005.3   Programs

The term *program* is used here rather than *software* because comprehensive works on software and firmware may be classed here. Firmware by itself, however, should be classed at 005.6.

Class a program or programs designed to run on two types of computers with the smaller type, e.g., a program for minicomputers and microcomputers 005.369.

Class programs for a specific application in computer science with the application in 005–006, but never in 004. Among the numbers most frequently used for software besides 005.3 and its subdivisions are 005.43 for systems software and operating systems, 005.71 for interfacing and data communications programs, 005.74 for database management systems, and 006.68 for computer graphics programs.

Beware: programs applied to a particular subject or discipline are classed with the subject or discipline, using s.s. 028553, e.g., programs for tax accounting 657.46028553.

See also — 00285; 005.1 vs. 005.3.

005.30218   Standards [of programs]

See 005.1 vs. 005.3.

005.30287   Testing and measurement [of programs]

See 005.1 vs. 005.3.

005.322   [Programs] In specific programming languages

Class here (and in cognate numbers) programs and works about programs only if the material being classified emphasizes the programming language. For much off-the-shelf software, the user does not need to know in what programming language it was written; such software is classed in 005.3 and its subdivisions other than those for programs in specific programming languages (and cognates of these numbers).

005.329   Specific programs

Class here (and in cognate numbers) programs having interdisciplinary applications, such as electronic spreadsheets (which can be used in research, business, personal finance, indeed any time a matrix format is useful) and statistics packages that are used more widely than just in research and that have report formatting or other features beyond statistical capabilities. If a work discussing how to use such a program is a guide that would be helpful to users applying the program in many fields, class it in 005.329 and cognate numbers even if most of the examples come from one field. If a work truly focuses on how to use such a program in a particular field, however, class it with that field, using s.s. 02855329 and cognate numbers, e.g., use of a particular electronic spreadsheet in financial administration 658.1502855329. In case of doubt, prefer 005.329 and cognate numbers.

005.43   Systems programs   Operating systems

Although there are technical differences between text editors and word processing programs, they are treated as the same for classification. Both are classed in 652.5.

005.6   Microprogramming and microprograms

Microprogramming does not mean programming for microcomputers, nor does *microprogram* mean a program for a microcomputer. *Microprogramming* means writing programs in which each instruction specifies a minute operation of the computer. Such programs are microprograms. Class programming for microcomputers in 005.26, programs for microcomputers in 005.36.

See also 004 vs. 005; 004–006 vs. 621.39.

005.71   Data communications

An example of a program for data communications is one that enables a user with a microcomputer and a modem to transmit and receive data and possibly also to store and manipulate data. The program may also prepare a computer to handle different forms of data, change transmission speeds to suit the hardware, store phone numbers and provide automatic routines so that the user need not repeat the connect process, etc.

See also 004 vs. 005; 004–006 vs. 621.39.

005.74   Data files and databases

Although there are technical differences between data files and databases, they are treated as the same for classification.

Class in 005.74 computer-science aspects of databases — that is, the narrowly technical issues of designing, programming, and installing databases and database management systems — the kinds of things that system designers and programmers need to know but that users generally do not need to know unless they are installing a database on their own computer. Class the subject content of databases (and works discussing that content) as if the databases were books, e.g., encyclopedic databases 030, bibliographic databases 010, non-bibliographic chemistry databases 540. Do not use s.s. 0285574 except for works that focus on the computer-science aspects of the databases rather than the subject content. Class guides to databases in 010, e.g., a guide to medical databases 016.61. Class in 025.04 the information science aspects of the automated storage and retrieval systems that make databases available—the kinds of things that users need to know about the systems in order to benefit fully from them. Class in 025.06 the information science aspects of the automated systems that make databases on specific subjects available to users.

005.74068 **Management of data files, of databases**

Do not use s.s. 068 for file management or database management in the sense of computer programs that enable operation of files or databases. Use s.s. 068 only for management of organizations, e.g., management of marketing in a firm that sells databases 005.740688.

005.82 vs. 652.8   Data encryption vs. Cryptography

Class in 005.82 cryptographic techniques used to limit access to information in computer systems, including computer networks. Class in 652.8 cryptographic techniques used to limit access to information not in computer systems. Class works treating both subjects in 652.8.

006.37 vs. **006.42, 621.367,** 621.391, and 621.399   Computer vision vs. **Optical pattern recognition, Technological photography and photooptics,** General works on [engineering of] specific types of computers, [and] Devices for special computer methods

Computer vision and optical pattern recognition both involve recognition of forms, shapes, or other optical patterns for the purpose of classification, grouping, or identification; but computer vision makes extensive use of artificial intelligence for the complex interpretation of visual information, whereas optical pattern recognition involves only simple interpretation.

Most works on computer vision and optical pattern recognition give substantial treatment to the computer programs needed to interpret optical patterns; such works are classed in 006.37 and 006.42, as are also works treating computer-vision and optical-pattern-recognition devices from the user's point of view. Class at 621.399 works on designing and manufacturing the hardware for computer vision and optical pattern recognition.

Class in 621.367 works on devices that record and process optical signals while doing virtually no interpreting (either because interpretation is not needed or because interpretation is left to others—computers or humans), e.g., devices for image enhancement.

At 621.391 *optical computer* refers to general-purpose computers in which the central data processing mechanism is based on light (e.g., lasers). Sometimes *optical computer* is used for special-purpose computers designed to process optical data, regardless of the type of central data processing mechanism. Works on such computers are classed in 006.37, 006.42, or 621.399.

006.42   Optical pattern recognition

See 006.37 vs. 006.42, 621.367, 621.391, and 621.399.

006.62   [Computer graphics] Hardware

Class here equipment specifically designed for computer graphics, such as color graphics terminals, and works treating use of equipment for computer graphics (even if the equipment was not specifically designed for that purpose). Class works that treat equally the use of equipment for graphics and non-graphics tasks in 004.

025.04   Information storage and retrieval systems

See 005.74.

384.3 vs. 004.6   **Computer communications vs. Interfacing and communications**

Class economic and related aspects of providing computer communications services to the public in 384.3. Class computer communications and its hardware in office and personal use, computer science applied to the technological aspects of computer communications, and interdisciplinary works in 004.6. If in doubt, prefer 004.6.

384.30285   **[Data processing, computer applications in computer communications]**

Class computer science applied to economic and related aspects of providing computer communications to the public in 384.3 and its subdivisions, using s.s. 0285, e.g., computer programs for analyzing economic and management aspects of interactive videotex 384.354028553.

See also 384.3 vs. 004.6.

384.31   Economic aspects [of computer communications]

Class economic aspects of production of computer communications hardware and software and comprehensive works on production and sale in 338.470046. Class sale of computer communications hardware and software in 380.1450046.

384.34   Electronic mail

See 384.352.

384.352   Broadcast videotex (Teletext)

Teletex is not the same as teletext (teletex: an electronic-mail system linking telex terminals, word processors, computer terminals; teletext: a system for transmitting computer-based information in coded form within the standard television signal for display on visual display units or television). Class teletex in 384.34.

620.004250285   **[Data processing   Computer applications in engineering design]**

See 670.285.

621.367   **Technological photography and photooptics**

See 006.37 vs. 006.42, 621.367, 621.391, and 621.399; 778.3 vs. 621.367.

621.38173   Microelectronic circuits

See 621.395 vs. 621.38173.

621.39   **[Engineering of] Computers**

Please note that 621.39 and its subdivisions were vacated in *Decimal Classification Additions, Notes and Decisions (DC&)* 4:4. The subdivisions still in use prior to publication of that *DC&* (621.393, 621.394, and 621.396) have not been reused in this new schedule.

See also 004–006 vs. 621.39.

621.391   General works on [engineering of] specific types of computers

See 006.37 vs. 006.42, 621.367, 621.391, and 621.399.

621.3911–   **Digital computers**
621.3916   *See 004.11–004.16.*

621.392   Systems analysis and design, computer architecture, performance evaluation

See 004–006 vs. 621.39; 004.21 vs. 004.22 and 621.392.

621.395 vs.   [Computer] Circuitry vs. Microelectronic circuits
   621.38173   Very-large-scale-integration (VLSI) is used primarily in computers, and most works on VLSI treat exclusively or predominately VLSI for computers. Many such works take the application to computers for granted, however, and do not emphasize it in their titles or front matter. Class here works on VLSI that do not emphasize how it will be applied. Class applications of VLSI in other fields with the application. If a work is found that treats VLSI in a variety of applications, and no one application predominates, class the work in 621.38173.

621.3981   [Engineering of] Interfacing and communications devices

See 004.6.

621.399   Devices for special computer methods

              See 006.37 vs. 006.42, 621.367, 621.391, and 621.399.

651.8   **Data processing   Computer applications [in office services]**

              See — 0285.

652.5   Word processing

              See 005.43.

652.8   Cryptography

              See 005.82 vs. 652.8.

658.05   **Data processing   Computer applications [in management]**

              See — 0285, 670.285.

670.285   **[Data processing   Computer applications in manufactures]**

Computer-aided design (CAD) is classed in 620.004250285 even if only manufactured goods are being designed, because topics in 620.1-620.9 applied to manufacturing in general are classed in 620. Computer-aided manufacture (CAM) refers primarily to automation of factory operations and is classed at 670.427. Computer use in the management of manufacturing is classed in 658.05. A work on any two of these topics (e.g., CAD/CAM) is not classed according to the usual first-of-two rule; rather, it is classed in 670.285.

670.427   Mechanization and automation of factory operations

              See 670.285.

Glossary

Analogue computers

Computers that represent variables by physical analogies, that is, translate physical conditions such as flow, temperature, or pressure into related mechanical or electronic circuits as an analogue for the physical phenomenon being investigated. The inputs and outputs of analogue computers are continuous signals, not discrete ones as in digital computers. (Note: An example of a continuous signal is the continuously changing time on a traditional watch with hands. On a digital watch, the time changes every second [or every minute or whatever the time unit is for a particular watch]; in the intervals between these discrete changes, the digital watch shows no change.)

Analogue-to-digital converters

Devices that measure analogue signals and convert them into digital signals. Analogue signals are continuous signals from devices that measure real-world phenomena such as temperature, sound, air quality. Digital signals are discrete signals conveying binary coded information that can be accepted by digital computers. See also **Analogue computers, Digital computers.**

Application generators

Software that produces a program to perform a task from the formalized description of that task.

Application programming

Writing application programs (q.v.).

Application programs

A comprehensive term for all kinds of programs designed to teach, entertain, or perform other tasks for users (such as information retrieval, payroll, statistical analysis). For the contrasting term, see **Systems programs.**

Artificial intelligence

The use of computers and related mechanisms for the solution of problems involving reasoning; the study of computer and related techniques to supplement the intellectual capabilities of human beings.

Assemblers

Programs that translate assembly-language statements into machine-code statements, which the processor can execute.

Assembly language

A programming language that uses mnemonic instructions (e.g., STO for store) instead of the binary numbers used in machine-language instructions. One assembly-language statement corresponds to one machine-language statement. An assembly language is designed to correspond to a specific computer's machine language.

Associative (Content-addressable) memory
Memory in which data is stored and retrieved according to content rather than location or address.

Associative processing
Parallel processing in which all data items may be searched simultaneously; data items are stored and retrieved based on all or part of their content.

Auxiliary storage see **External (Auxiliary) storage.**

Bar-code scanning
Using optical wands or other devices to read codes in the form of bars of varying thickness that represent characters (numerals, letters, etc.).

Baseband
In computer communications, refers to a channel with a relatively small bandwidth that cannot transmit as much data as quickly as a broadband channel, nor can it transmit beyond two or three miles. It can carry only digital signals.

Batch processing
Grouping of similar transactions for processing during the same machine run.

Bipolar memory
Semiconductor memory employing bipolar junction transistors. These transistors have two poles and two current carriers.

Broadband
In computer communications, refers to a channel with a relatively large bandwidth that can transmit large amounts of data quickly over long distances. Both analogue and digital signals may be carried over broadband channels.

Broadcast videotex (Teletext)
A system for transmitting computer-based information in coded form within the standard television signal for display on visual display units or television.

Bubble memory see **Magnetic bubble memory.**

Central processing units (CPUs)
Those parts of computers containing the circuitry to perform all the arithmetic, logic, and control operations.

Centralized databases
Databases that are the only databases in their system and that receive data or are searched from multiple locations.

Centralized processing
Processing at one central location obtained from several physical locations.

Code generator
Part of a programming-language translator, such as a compiler. A code generator takes programs already analyzed (parsed, etc.) and produces assembly-language or machine-language code.

Coding of programs
Representing programs in a symbolic form that can be accepted by a data processor.

Communications network architecture
Design of a communications system, including the choice of hardware, software, and communications protocols to be used in the system.

Communications protocols
Procedures and formats allowing computers (or computers and terminals) to exchange information.

Compilers
Programs that translate high-level languages (q.v.) into a language acceptable to a computer.

Computer architecture
Design and organization of computers.

Computer communications
Transfer of computer-based information by any of various media (e.g., coaxial cable or radio waves) from one computer to another or between computers and terminals.

Computer communications networks
Systems of communications channels linking two or more computers or computers and terminals. Various channels may be used, e.g., microwave, optical fibers, coaxial cables.

Computer operating systems see **Operating systems.**

Computer peripherals
Input, output, and storage devices that work with a computer but are not part of its central processing unit or internal storage. They may be enclosed within the same frame as the central processing unit.

Computer systems
1. Computers, their peripheral devices, and their operating systems or master control programs.
2. Systems consisting of more than a single computer; computer networks.
3. Organized sets of computer programs that work together (application or systems programs).

Computer vision
Computer processing, categorizing, and understanding of visual information, using artificial intelligence, e.g., identifying types and positions of industrial parts.

Content-addressable memory see **Associative (Content-addressable) memory.**

Core memory see **Magnetic-core memory.**

CPU (Central processing unit) see **Central processing units (CPUs).**

Data bases see **Databases.**

Data communications see **Computer communications.**

Data compaction see **File (Data) compression.**

Data compression see **File (Data) compression.**

Data dictionaries
Repositories of information about data, containing the name of each data element, its definition (size and type), where and how it is used and its relationships to the other data, but not containing the actual data. Usually combined with data directories (q.v.).

Data directories
Repositories of information about the location of data and how it can be accessed, not containing the actual data. Usually combined with data dictionaries (q.v.).

Data encryption
Converting data from a standard digital code to a special code for security purposes. In this process the information is scrambled according to predefined rules so that it cannot be read without knowledge of those rules.

Data entry
Putting data into a computer system.

Data files
Organized collections of records, the collections being treated as units. The information in the records may consist of characters, numbers, symbols, or combinations of these. Among the types of data files are numeric files, text files, and graphics files.

Data representation
The encoded machine-readable form in which data is recorded.

Data security
Techniques involved in preventing unauthorized access to data and unauthorized or accidental modification or destruction of data.

Data structures
Forms of logical organization of records in a file (e.g., arrays, lists, tables, trees).

Data validation
Techniques to verify the reliability of data, e.g., tests for incorrect characters.

Database machines
Computers dedicated to handling the loading of data into and retrieval of data from a database.

Database management systems
Computer programs that enable operation of a database, e.g., by indexing, retrieving, and updating records, and duplicating the database as a backup.

Databases

Integrated collections of interrelated records or files that can be accessed using various search keys (e.g., author or subject headings).

Debugging

Correcting (removing the "bugs" from) a computer program that is not working properly or (less often) correcting malfunctions in a computer or computer peripheral.

Digital codes

Sets of rules defining the way in which bits can be arranged to represent numbers, letters, and special symbols in a computer, e.g., ASCII (American Standard Code for Information Interchange).

Digital computers

Computers that perform their tasks by noting the presence or absence of physical signals in a particular position. This on or off condition represents binary data that can be manipulated arithmetically or logically to produce a solution. The inputs and outputs of digital computers are discrete signals, not continuous signals as in analogue computers. Most computers today are digital computers. See also **Analogue computers.**

Digital-to-analogue converters

Devices that convert digital signals into the corresponding analogue signals. See also **Analogue computers, Analogue-to-digital converters, Digital computers.**

Digitizer tablets

Flat tablets that serve as drawing surfaces for graphics input.

Distributed databases

Databases located at different locations in a system rather than centrally located.

Distributed processing

Processing data at different locations in a system of computers connected by a communications network.

Editors

1. Linkage editors are systems programs that combine into one module a number of program segments that have been independently compiled or assembled.
2. Text editors are programs that allow users to enter, alter, format and store program and manuscript text.

Electronic mail

Electronic transmission of letters, messages, and memos through a communications network. *Electronic mail* most commonly refers to communications using computers and computer terminals, but in its broadest sense it includes also telex and facsimile transmission.

Ergonomic engineering

Designing machinery for comfortable, effective interaction with people (e.g., making video display screens that are easy to read and do not irritate the eyes).

Error-correcting codes
Codes that assist in restoration of a word or other data that has been mutilated in transmission.

Expert systems
Knowledge-based systems (q.v.) designed to operate at the expert level.

External (Auxiliary) storage
Storage devices separate from a computer's primary storage but holding information in a form acceptable to the computer, for example, machine-readable disks and tapes.

File (Data) compression
Techniques to save space and time required for storage, processing, and transmission of data, e.g., by eliminating gaps and redundancies or by changing from binary to hexadecimal coding.

File processing
Operations performed on files, e.g., updating.

Files see **Data files**.

Firmware
Programs written in microcode (q.v.) and more or less permanently stored in computer chips.

Formal languages
Abstract mathematical constructs used to model the syntax of programming languages, or natural languages, such as English.

Hierarchical databases
Databases with a structure that allows a record of one type to be related to 0 to n records of another type, e.g., a customer record may be linked to no, one, or multiple current order records. Each record type may be involved in only one relationship as a subordinate (e.g., a current order record can be linked to only one customer record), and only one relationship is allowed between any two record types.

High-level languages
Programming languages that are closer to natural languages and farther from machine language than are low-level languages or assembly languages. BASIC and FORTRAN are examples of high-level languages.

High-speed local networks
Networks designed for communication among high-speed devices such as mainframe computers and mass storage devices at one computing site.

Hybrid computers
Computers that are combinations of analogue and digital computers linked together by interface systems that convert analogue data to digital data and vice versa.

Interactive processing

Processing in which each user input elicits a response, and there is a continuous dialog between user and computer.

Interactive videotex (Viewdata)

A system for transmitting computer-based information by cable (e.g., television lines) for display on visual display units or television sets, with a capacity for interactive, two-way communication between the computer and the receiving unit.

Interfacing

Equipment and techniques linking computers to peripheral devices or to other computers.

Internal storage (Main memory)

The primary storage space in a computer, where data is stored for rapid retrieval by the central processing unit.

Interpreters

Programs that translate and execute each statement of a program before translating and executing the next statement.

Job-control languages

Command languages that tell a computer's operating system how a job should be run.

Knowledge-based systems

Computer systems in which artificial-intelligence programs utilize inference and heuristic procedures and databases of knowledge (knowledge bases) in order to solve problems. See also **Expert systems.**

Linkage editors see **Editors.**

Local-area networks

Computer communications networks that operate over a small area, e.g., one site (or several nearby sites) of a company.

Machine language

A language that is used directly by a computer; it consists of a sequence of binary patterns.

Machine learning

The process by which a computer may improve its performance based on prior executions of the same program.

Macro processor

Software to translate macroinstructions (q.v.). A macro processor translates each macroinstruction into the sequence of instructions for which it stands. Then a compiler or assembler can translate these instructions into machine code.

Macroinstructions

Computer instructions, each of which stands for a given sequence of instructions.

Magnetic bubble memory
A solid-state memory device involving microscopic magnetized areas, called "bubbles," in thin films of magnetic material. The presence or absence of a bubble in a particular location can be used to denote a binary digit.

Magnetic-core memory
Primary storage consisting of tiny magnetic rings—the most common type of primary storage in computers of the 1960s.

Main memory see **Internal storage (Main memory).**

Main storage see **Internal storage (Main memory).**

Mainframe computers
Large computers, as distinguished from minicomputers or microcomputers. (Used with its original meaning, *mainframe* refers to the piece of equipment that contains the central processing unit.)
See also *Manual* 004.11–004.16.

Memory see **External (Auxiliary) storage, Internal storage (Main memory).**

Metal-oxide-semiconductor (MOS) memories
Memories employing field-effect transistors (FET). Layers of metal, oxide, and semiconductor form the gate structure of these transistors. These transistors require only a single pole and one current carrier, by contrast to the transistors used in bipolar memories.

Microassembly languages
Languages that express microcode (q.v.) instructions in symbolic form.

Microcode
Microinstructions stored in more or less permanent memory to control the operation of a computer. Each microinstruction activates a specific circuit in the computer to perform part of the operation specified by a machine-language instruction.

Microcomputers
Small, relatively low-cost computers having central processing units contained on single chips (or occasionally more than one chip). These central processing units are called microprocessors.
See also *Manual* 004.11–004.16.

Microprocessors
Central processing units (q.v.) of microcomputers.

Microprogramming
Writing programs in which each instruction specifies a minute operation of the computer.

Minicomputers
Intermediate-sized computers, between microcomputers and mainframes. Minicomputers generally operate at about twice the speed of microcomputers.
See also *Manual* 004.11–004.16.

Modems

Devices for converting digital signals into analogue signals by modulation, and for converting analogue signals to digital signals by demodulation.

Modular programming

A technique of programming whereby a program is divided into separate units or modules, each of which has clearly defined functions and interfaces. The modules are programmed and tested separately, then merged and tested as a unit.

Monitors

1. Video display screens.
2. Various kinds of programs that control the operation of a computer.

Multiplexing

Transmitting multiple signals over a single channel.

Multiprocessing

Executing two or more programs concurrently, using two or more interconnected processors.

Multiprogramming

Running two or more programs in one computer at the same time.

Network architecture see **Communications network architecture.**

Network databases

Databases in which essentially no restrictions are placed on the number and type of relationships among types of records.

Nonprocedural languages

Computer programming languages that allow a programmer to state the goals to be achieved without giving details about how they are to be achieved—that is, without giving as many details as would be required with procedural languages. *Nonprocedural* is a relative term.

Offline processing

Processing using equipment not under the direct control of the central processing unit.

Online processing

1. Processing in which terminals, disks, and other peripheral equipment are connected to the central processor and ready for use, so that there is no need for human intervention between user input and computer response.
2. Processing transactions in random order, without waiting to collect a batch of similar transactions.

Operating systems

Master control programs that supervise the sequencing and processing of programs by a computer and which may provide additional services, such as debugging, input-output control, storage assignment.

Optical computers
Computers in which the central data processing mechanism is based on light (e.g., lasers). These may be general- or special-purpose computers.

Packet switching
A method of routing a message in a network by which the message is broken into small units, called *packets*. Each packet is sent to the destination by the most expedient route, with different parts of the same message possibly traveling by different routes. The destination computer reassembles the packets into the message.

Parallel processing
Executing two or more programs concurrently, using two or more interconnected processors that are active at the same time on the same program.

Parsers
Programs to analyze the syntax of a programming-language statement so as to decipher what a programmer has requested.

Pattern recognition
Computer recognition of forms, shapes, or other patterns in any sort of input (e.g., visual, tactile, acoustic, chemical, electrical) for the purpose of classification, grouping, or identification.

Perceptrons
Machines that have light-sensing receptors analogous to the retina of the eye and that determine whether an object fits a certain pattern by doing mathematical calculations on the patterns of light received in the receptors.

Peripheral control units
Intermediary control devices that regulate the transfer of data between central processing units and peripheral devices.

Peripherals see **Computer peripherals.**

Pipeline processing
Processing in which certain computer operations are overlapped to increase processing speed, e.g., by executing one instruction at the same time that the next instruction is being fetched from memory.

Plotters
Graphics output machines that draw lines with ink pens.

Processors
1. Central processing units (q.v.).
2. Language processors see **Translators.**

Program design
The phase of programming in which the program logic is worked out, before the program is coded.

Programming-language translators see **Translators.**

Programs

Software (q.v.) and firmware (q.v.), which consist of instructions to direct the operation of a computer or its peripheral equipment. Groups of instructions make up programs.

Random-access memory (RAM)

Temporary memory chip, the contents being lost when power is turned off.

Read-only memory (ROM)

Permanent memory chip for program storage. The program can be read from the chip, but no new information can be stored in it.

Real-time processing

Immediate processing with little delay in computer response to user input.

Relational databases

Databases in which data is perceived by users as organized into arrays of rows and columns (the rows are records, and the columns are fields); and relationships between two record types are expressed implicitly by inclusion of certain data items in both records (e.g., a supplier code in both a supplier record and a purchase-order record).

Semiconductor bipolar memory see **Bipolar memory.**

Software

Instructions to direct the operation of a computer or its peripherals. Groups of instructions make up programs. Software, as distinct from firmware, is not permanently stored in computer chips.

Software engineering

Techniques for development of software, encompassing all stages of development.

Software maintenance

Work done on a program after it has been released for normal use.

Structured programming

A collection of techniques designed to make programming more rigorous. These may include restricting the numbers and kinds of program structures (e.g., avoiding GO-TO structures), allowing only one entrance and one exit, producing documentation and doing testing at every stage of the software development cycle.

Supercomputers

Computers that are faster and have higher computing capacity than standard mainframe computers.

See also *Manual* 004.11–004.16.

System

1. Set of components that can be seen as working together for the overall objectives of the whole.
2. Operating system.
3. Computer system.

See also **Systems programs.**

Systems programming
Writing systems programs (q.v.).

Systems programs
Programs that do not directly perform users' tasks but that enable a computer and its peripherals to operate so that programs to carry out users' tasks may be executed. For the contrasting term, see **Application programs.**

Teletex
An electronic-mail system linking telex terminals, word processors, computer terminals.

Teletext see **Broadcast videotex (Teletext).**

Text editors see **Editors.**

Text processing
Computer processing of information coded as characters or sequences of characters (as contrasted with information coded as numbers). Text processing includes word processing, but it also includes everything else that computers can do by manipulating characters, e.g., counting word frequency, making concordances, storing and retrieving text.

Thin-film memory
Primary storage made by depositing extremely thin films of a magnetizable material on an insulating base, such as glass.

Time sharing
A method by which a number of users may use the computer at the same time, usually interactively. Each user is allotted a proportion of processing time, and the computer services each user in sequence, switching at high speed from one user to the next. If the system works well, it may appear that all the users are being handled simultaneously.

Translators
Programs that allow programmers to write programs in a language closer to natural language than a machine could understand. Translators convert programs written in a programming language into a language acceptable by a machine (or by another translator, which completes the conversion).

Utility programs
Systems programs that perform "housekeeping" tasks required by many users, e.g., transferring information from one medium to another (card-to-disk, disk-to-print, etc.), providing statistics on disk space.

Value-added network services
Communications networks that provide services in addition to communication channels, such as automatic error detection and correction, protocol conversion.

Videotex see **Broadcast videotex, Interactive videotex (Viewdata).**

Viewdata see **Interactive videotex (Viewdata).**

Virtual memory

Method of expanding the available storage of a computer by transferring information one page or more at a time between internal and external storage, so that a program can be executed even though not all of it can fit into internal memory at one time.

Wide-area networks

Computer communications networks that span a large geographical area, e.g., a state, nation, or continent.

Corrections, Changes, and New Numbers

1. Edition 19

Volume 1

p. 5   −028 5   *In heading make 2 changes:*

Delete: [*formerly also* −0183]

Add: Computer applications

Delete notes and substitute:

The subdivisions of this standard subdivision are new and have been prepared with little or no reference to previous editions. Most numbers have been reused with new meanings

Class here selection and use of computer hardware, comprehensive works on hardware and programs in electronic data processing, electronic computers, electronic digital computers, computer systems, central processing units, computer reliability

Unless it is redundant, add to base number −0285 the numbers following 00 in 004–006, e.g., digital microcomputers −0285416, but digital computers −0285 (*not* −02854)

p. 473   004   *Add heading:*

Data processing   Computer science

p. 473   005   *Add heading:*

Computer programming, programs, data

p. 473   006   *Add heading:*

Special computer methods

Volume 2

p. 1   SUMMARY   *At .6 delete line*

p. 3	001.534	*Delete 2nd and 3rd notes and substitute:*

Class computer pattern recognition in 006.4, computer optical character recognition in 006.424 [*both formerly also* 001.534]

Class psychology of perception in 153.7

p. 4	001.535	*Delete heading and substitute:* Automata theory

Delete notes and substitute:

Class artificial intelligence [*formerly* 001.535] in 006.3

p. 5	001.6	*Bracket:* [.6]

Delete note and substitute: Class in 004

p. 5	001.61	*Delete this entry and the following 13 entries*
p. 7	003	*In 2nd note change* 001.61 *to:* 004.21
p. 563	SUMMARY	*At .4 delete line and substitute:*

.3 Computer communications

p. 564	384.1	*Insert as 1st note:*

Class here submarine cable telegraphy [*formerly* 384.4]

In 2nd note delete:

; submarine cable telegraphy, 384.4

p. 564	384.14	*Add to 2nd note:*

, comprehensive works on electronic mail in 384.34

p. 564   *Insert 8 new entries:*

.3   Computer communications

Transfer of computer-based information by any of various media (e.g., coaxial cable or radio waves) from one computer to another or between computers and terminals

Class here links between computers via telephone lines [*formerly* 384.648], computer communications networks

Class interdisciplinary works on computer communications in 004.6

.31   Economic aspects

Market, supply and demand, costs, rates, finance, income, efficiency, competition

Class economic aspects of facilities in 384.32, of services in 384.33

.32   Facilities

Class use of facilities in specific services in 384.33

.33   Services

Including services of value-added networks

For electronic mail, see 384.34; videotex, 384.35

.34   Electronic mail

Including teletex

Class here electronic mail using computers or computers and computer terminals, comprehensive works on electronic mail

Class specific kinds of electronic mail with the kind, e.g., postal facsimile transmission 383.141, telex 384.14

.35   Videotex

.352   Broadcast videotex (Teletext)

.354   Interactive videotex (Viewdata)

p. 564	384.4	*Bracket:* [.4] *Delete note and substitute:* Class in 384.1
p. 567	384.648	*Bracket:* [.648] *Delete notes and substitute:* Class in 384.3
p. 620	511.3	*Insert as 1st note:* Including Turing machines [*formerly* 621.381952], infinite-state machines [*formerly* 621.3819594]
p. 636	519.4	*In 1st note delete:* computer mathematics, *Insert as 2nd note:* Class computer mathematics [*formerly* 519.4] in 004.0151
p. 928	SUMMARY	*At .39 delete heading and substitute:* Computers
p. 941	621.381 7	*In 2nd note change number to:* 621.39
p. 942	621.381 95	*Bracket:* [.381 95] *Add note:* Class in 621.39
p. 942	621[.381 950 151]	*Delete this entry and the following 2 entries*
p. 942	621.381 952	*Bracket:* [.381 952] *Delete heading and substitute:* Turing machines *Delete notes (2nd note introduced in* DC& *4:3) and substitute:* Class in 511.3
p. 942	621.381 953	*Delete this entry and the following 15 entries*
p. 943	621.381 594	*Bracket:* [.381 954] *Delete heading and substitute:* Infinite-state machines *Delete note (introduced in* DC& *4:3) and substitute:* Class in 511.3

p. 943	621.381 959 6	*Delete this entry and the following entry*
p. 1030	629.891	*In note change number to:* 621.39
p. 1103	651[.028 5]	*Add to heading:* Computer applications
p. 1106	651.8	*Add to heading:* Computer applications

Insert as 1st note:

The subdivisions of this number are new and have been prepared with little or no reference to previous editions. Most numbers have been reused with new meanings

Add as 3rd note:

Unless it is redundant, add to base number 651.8 the numbers following 00 in 004–006, e.g., non-electronic data processing 651.849, use of digital microcomputers 651.8416, but use of digital computers 651.8 (*not* 651.84)

p. 1106	651.81	*Delete this entry and the following 3 entries*
p. 1114	658 [.002 85]	*Add to heading:* Computer applications
p. 1114	658.05	*Add to heading:* Computer applications

Delete 1st note and substitute:

The subdivisions of this number are new and have been prepared with little or no reference to previous editions. Most numbers have been reused with new meanings

Unless it is redundant, add to base number 658.05 the numbers following 00 in 004–006, e.g., use of digital microcomputers 658.05416, but use of digital computers 658.05 (*not* 658.054)

p. 1197	681.14	*In 2nd note change number to:* 621.39

Volume 3

p. 71	Artificial intelligence cybernetics	*Delete* cybernetics 001.535 *and substitute:*
		computer science 006.3
p. 182	Character-recognition cybernetics	*Delete line and substitute:*
	computer science	006.4
	optical	006.424

p. 215	Code telegraphy		
	commun. ind.		
	commerce		
	wire		
	submarine cable	*Change number to:* 384.14	

p. 232	Computer		
	communications		
	telephony	*Delete this line and the following 4 lines and substitute:*	

	commerce	384.3
	govt. control	351.874 3
	spec. jur.	353–354
	law	
	international	341.757 7
	municipal	343.099 45
	spec. jur.	343.4–.9

| p. 232 | Computer | |
| | mathematics | *Change number to:* 004.015 1 |

p. 287	Demand	
	prod. econ.	
	commun. services	
	telecommunications	
	telegraphy	
	submarine cable	*Change number to:* 384.13

p. 336	Efficiency	
	prod. econ.	
	secondary ind.	
	communication	
	telegraphy	
	submarine cable	*Change number to:* 384.13

p. 395	Finance	
	prod. econ.	
	communication	
	commerce	
	telegraphy	
	submarine cable	*Change number to:* 384.13

| p. 527 | Infinite-state machines | *On same line add:* 511.3 |
| | electronic eng. | *Delete this line and the following 6 lines* |

p. 640	Markets	
	prod. econ.	
	commun. services	
	telecommunications	
	telegraphy	
	submarine cable	*Change number to:* 384.13
p. 751	Optical	
	character recognition	*On same line add:* 006.424
	cybernetics	*Delete line*
p. 764	Ownership	
	commun. systems	
	telegraphy	
	submarine cable	*Change number to:* 384.13
p. 786	Pattern-recognition	
	cybernetics	*Delete line and substitute:*
	computer science 006.4	
p. 857	Printing	
	telegraphy	
	commun. ind.	
	commerce	
	wire	
	submarine cable	*Change number to:* 384.14
p. 900	Rates	
	commun. ind.	
	commerce	
	telegraphy	
	submarine cable	*Change number to:* 384.13
p. 1061	Submarine	
	cable telegraphy	
	commerce	*Change number to:* 384.1
	govt. control	*Change number to:* 351.874 1
p. 1070	Supply	
	prod. econ.	
	commun. services	
	telecommunications	
	telegraphy	
	submarine cable	*Change number to:* 384.13

p. 1090   Telegraphy
   stations
    commun. ind.
     commerce
      wire
       submarine cable *Change number to:* 384.15

p. 1139   Turing machines   *Change number (introduced in* DC& *4:3) to:*
              511.3

2. Manual on the Use of the Dewey Decimal Classification: Edition 19

p. 31   001.61   *Delete this entry and the following 3 entries*

p. 334   **651.8**   *In note change number to:* 004

p. 441   001.6   *Delete entry*

p. 522   Input   *Delete entry*

p. 531   Output   *Delete entry*

p. 543   Storage   *Delete entry*

p. 545   Systems
      analysis   *Delete this line*